YOGA AND ZEN
A Monograph

YOGA AND ZEN

A Monograph

K.V. Raghupathi

SHARADA

Sharada Publishing House
Delhi - 110 085
2007

First Published 2007

ISBN: 81-88934-47-X

Published by
Anjana Bansal
SHARADA PUBLISHING HOUSE
111, Vidya Vihar Apartment
Sector - 9, Rohini, Delhi - 110 085
Ph.: +91-11-3292 1560, 2755 2102
E-mail: bansal_sph@rediffmail.com

Printed at
Salasar Imaging Process
Delhi -110 035

Contents

Preface

The basis of this monograph is a paper I presented at a national seminar on Yoga sponsored by Indian Council of Philosophical Research (ICPR), New Delhi and held in collaboration with the Department of Philosophy, S.V. University, Tirupati in February 22nd-24th, 2007. After presenting the paper, I thought that I should develop the theme into a well researched book form. But, yielding much to my second thoughts, I felt I should be content with taking its shape in a monograph. With my considerable experience in Yoga which I have been practicing in Patañjali's tradition and with my vast reading of books on Zen, I humbly believe that this fascinating comparative study would best yield results both for the general readers and practioners and academicians as well in the long run and I am confident this small but inestimable study would pave the way for the scholars to plunge deeply into these two unique systems that India has given as divine gifts to humanity.

The author is very much grateful to Mrs. Anjana Bansal of Sharada Publishing House for publishing this book within a short period.

Chapter I

The ancient India was broad based in spirituality. There were a broad range of spiritual pathways, miracle practices and beliefs. The Vedas came into existence around 2000 B.C. The Upaniṣads were given to humanity between 800 and 600 B.C. Then came different schools of philosophy (*darśanas*) which interpreted the Upaniṣadic texts, each in its own unique manner. Yoga was one such school which derived from Sāṁkhya system. Yoga is theistic, but distinct from other schools in respect of advocating eight fold path (*Āṣṭāṅga Yoga*). Yoga, in its simplistic manner, is understood as moving from the lower level of sense organs and mind to a higher plane of consciousness. There are many forms of Yoga, deviated from the original tenets of Patañjali's *Yoga Sūtras*. Yoga was one of the earliest practices to use meditation as its primary method. *Dhyāna* is the seventh limb in *Āṣṭāṅga Yoga*. It belongs to the higher form of Yoga, the lower being *Yama, Niyama, Āsana, Prāṇāyāma* and *Pratyahāra*. Patañjali's Yoga is evolutionary and not sudden. It involves eight steps, each leading to the other gradually.

It is both an evolutive path (*onward journey)* and involutive path (*inward journey*) in the quest of the soul. As time went by different schools within Yoga were born, each professing a different kind of path with modification.

Chapter II

Of the six systems (*Darśanas*), Vedānta and Yoga are considered to be the two highest systems, the former depicting the essence of truth and knowing; the latter offering a systematic methodology as to how to experience the former. The paramount importance of Yoga and place it occupies in Hindu philosophy is unquestionable and supreme. Mere theoretical knowledge and speculation without practical and direct experience is tantamount to nothing. The greatness of Yoga is duly recognized in the *Bhagavadgītā*. "The Yogī is greater than ascetics; he is greater than even the wise or *Jñānin;* he is greater than a man of action or rituals; become though a Yogin, O Arjuna ! (*Chapter 6, Verse* 46). In *Yājñavalkya Smṛti* it has been written that among sacrifies, customs, charity, the most important is the realization of the *Ātman* through Yoga. All knowledge is a thing of the mind. Yoga is also thing of the mind, but a much 'deeper thing' at a higher and highest levels: a mind deep in *Ātman*. Its importance is highlighted in texts such as *Viṣṇu Purāṇa, Skanda Purāṇa, Āditya Purāṇa* and *Yājñavalkya Saṁhitā.*

In a general sense any path that leads to realization of the Higher could be treated as Yoga. So, it takes different names which throw the mind of an aspirant into confusion and disarray. But, here, we are primarily dealing with the Yoga system as propounded by Patañjali. This Yoga tradition is rich, colourful, systematic, scientific and evolutionary. This system is much older than the so-called modern Haṭha Yoga traditions. The earliest Haṭha Yoga could be linked to the name of Gorakhanātha. He was considered to be the founder of the order of *Kanphaṭa Yogins*. He was historically placed by most authorities in the 12th century A.D. the treatise entitled *Haṭha Yoga* is said to have been lost and his other text *Gorakṣārthaka* too. The other three Haṭha Yoga classics, that came into existence much later than the Haṭha Yoga of Gorakhanātha include; *Haṭha Yoga Pradīpikā* of Svatmarama Svami, probably belonging to 15th century, *Śiva Saṁhitā* and *Gheraṇḍa Saṁhitā*, probably attributed to *Gheraṇḍa*, a Vaiṣṇavite of Bengal. Of these *Gheraṇḍa Saṁhitā* is considered to be a complete Yoga system. It is not simply Haṭha Yoga as it is understood by innumerable authorities. This Yoga is seven fold which includes purification, *Āsanas, Mudrās, Pratyahāra, Prāṇāyāma, Dhyāna* and *Samādhi*. It is known as *Saptāṅga Yoga* whereas in *Haṭhayoga Pradīpikā* it is *Caturaṅga Yoga*.

The philosophy of *Gheraṇḍa Saṁhitā* is put in the form of a dialogue between *Gheraṇḍa*, the preceptor and

Caṇḍakapālī, the disciple. It widely differs from *Haṭhayoga Pradīpikā* and the other texts on *Haṭha Yoga*. It does not use the word 'Haṭha' in the form of Yoga. The Yoga that has been discussed in *Gheraṇḍa Saṁhitā* is called 'Ghaṭastha Yoga'. 'Ghaṭa' is a technical word which indicates body. But it is more than 'body'. It includes *'Liṅga śarīra'* (Subtle body) that transmigrates and is responsible for another birth. It is responsible for good or evil actions which determine the further course of rebirth. This chain can be broken through the practice of Yoga known as *'Saptāṅga Yoga'*. The process by which purification is done is known as *'Ghaṭa Śuddhi'*. But it is not only purification but also fortification of the psycho-physical unit. The Ghaṭa Śuddhi which takes place through *Saptāṅga Yoga* consisting of *Ṣaṭ Karmas: Āsana, Mudrā, Pratyahāra, Prāṇāyāma, Dhyāna* and *Samādhi* is known as *Ghaṭastha Yoga* in *Gheraṇḍa Saṁhitā*. It describes 102 Yogic practices which can be classified as *Kriyās* (21), *Āsanas* (32), *Mudrās* (25), *Pratyahāras* (5), *Prāṇayāmas* (10), *Dhyānas* (3) and *Samādhis* (6). In these Yogic practices there is a gradual evolution of the process from physical to metaphysical (spiritual) through psychological.

Haṭhayoga Pradīpikā, the name by itself obviously refers to physical. Many have mistaken the text for dealing with only physical. This is a tremendous misconception, B.K.S. Iyengar, an authoritarian on *Haṭha Yoga* observes. Taking the etymological meaning of 'Haṭha', 'Ha' means sun and 'ṭha' means moon. The sun could be here treated as representing consciousness, ever shining and the moon mind and body, ever changing and unstable. Hence, the union between the two is Yoga. Further, the last chapter of the text is called *Samādhi Pāda* which speaks of the state of *Samādhi*. The text also says that Yoga is '*Prāṇa Vṛtti Nirōdha*' (Stilling the fluctuations of breath), whereas Patañjali's *Yoga Sūtras* says that *Yoga* is "*Citta Vṛtti Nirōdha*" (stilling the fluctuations of the mind). Yet both meet at a certain point and there is ultimately no difference between them.

Patañjali's eight-limb system "(*Āṣṭāṅga Yoga*) is, however, considered to be the most authenticated, venerable, acclaimed and recognized system of Yoga. Prior to Patañjali Yoga was practiced in varied forms in different regions with having no clear cut vision, direction and methodology. It was Patañjali, some two thousand five hundred years ago, organized it in a scientific way and expounded it in his magnum opus treatise, *Yoga Sūtras* which contain four sections consisting of one hundred and ninety six *Sūtras* or aphorisms. This text of *Sūtras* stands out as the most authoritative and useful book. In these one hundred and ninety six *Sūtras*, Patañjali has condensed the essential philosophy and technique of Yoga in a marvelous way. The first experience of reading these pithy sayings would give a vague impression and understanding. But a more careful and deeper study of the words in the *Sūtrās* will reveal the profound meaning and rational basis with which the whole technique is treated.

The first section named as *Samādhi Pāda* consisting of 51 *Sūtras* primarily deals with the nature of *Samādhi*, much elaborately since *Samādhi* is the essential technique of Yoga. In the second *Sūtra* he defines 'what is Yoga?' as "*Yogaḥ Citta Vṛtti Nirōdhaḥ*" that is, "Yoga is the control of the modifications of mind." This indeed is the crux of this section as well as the entire text. For the first time, more than two millennia ago, Patañjali systematically studied and examined the nature of the mind and described the front brain as the analytical brain, the back brain as the reasoning brain, the bottom brain as the seat of bliss and the top brain as the creative brain or the seat of individuality. The bottom brain incidentally corresponds to the hypothalamus as described by the modern science.

Patañjali introduces the ways of stilling the mind which is essential for experiencing the higher consciousness. In the second part of this section, Patañjali draws our attention to the nature of *Samādhi* which occupies the most important position among other topics dealt with. This Section is not for all but for the advanced *Sādhakas* who have attained the state of even mind in all circumstances.

The second section named as *Sādhanā Pāda* consisting of 55 *Sūtras* is meant for the beginners who want to tread the path of Yoga. The first part of this section 1 to 28 *Sūtras* deals with the philosophy of *Kleśas* and Patañjali gives a masterly treatment to the conditions of human life and the misery and suffering which are inherent in these conditions. Also, the first *Sūtra* of this Section deals with what *Kriyā Yoga* is. It reads as : *Tapaḥ – Svādhyāyeśvara – Praṇidhanāmi kriyā yogaḥ*, that is, austerity (self-discipline), self study and surrender to god together contribute the Yoga of action.

The second part of this section deals with the first five limbs of *Āṣṭāṅga Yoga*. (*Yama, Niyama, Āsana, Prāṇāyāma,* and *Pratyahāra*) which are referred to as *Bahiraṅga* or external. These practices are made mandatory for the beginners who want to move to the higher. These are of a preparatory nature and meant to make the *Sādhakas* fit for the practice of *Dhāraṇa, Dhyāna* and *Samādhi*.

The third section consisting of 56 *Sūtras* is called *Vibhūti Pāda*. In the first part of the section Patañjali deals with the three remaining limbs of yogic technique which are referred to as *Antaraṅga* or internal. The three taken together constitute *Saṁyama (Trayaṃ ekatra saṁyamaḥ, Sūtra:* 4). It is through these techniques, the mysteries of Yogic life are unravelled and the powers or *Siddhis* are acquired. Patañjali describes thirty five powers which might be experienced if one practices the Yoga with sincerity, devotion and perseverance. These powers and gifts, Patañjali says, may become traps for the practitioners if non-attachment is not practiced. They may distract the harmony and prevent the practitioners from proceeding further.

In the Forth and the last section titled as *Kaivalya Pāda* consisting of 34 *Sūtras* Patañjali expounds all those essential philosophical problems which are involved in the study and practice of Yoga. The nature of mind, its complexity of forming desires and craving for them, their effects are dealt with briefly but systematically to enable the practitioner to have an adequate background of theoretical knowledge. Besides, the nature of *Kaivalya* (absolute liberation) constitutes the subject of this section. When extraordinary powers are subdued in great humility, the *Sādhaka* can climb the ladder and finally be freed from the bondage of body, mind and world and enter into *Kaivalya.*

Patañjali's *Yoga Sūtras* is the most comprehensive and systematic and suitable treatise for deep and systematic study of Yoga. The text provides not only theoretical knowledge which is considered a must for the practioners so as not to fall but also practical problems encountered in the *Sādhana.* It gives all the essential information about Yoga in a masterly but scientific manner. It is not simply treated as a religion or a dogma or a creed, but provides a way of life – a life that could be properly understood, its meaning, significance and value in the matrix of cosmic creation, a life that could be trodden not merely for gaining powers or *Kaivalya,* though it constitutes the ultimate goal, but simply to lead a life of harmony, peace and happiness. It is for this reason *Yoga Sūtras* is recognized as a masterpiece in the literature of Yoga and has withstood the test of time over two thousand years.

There can be no doubt that a serious pursuit of this path is ridden with full of thorns, and cannot be undertaken as a hobby or to find a mere palliative for the modern life of stress and strain. The text with 196 *Sūtras* provides a deep insight into the understanding of human nature in its gamut and the misery and suffering inherent in it and thereby out of it is the disciplined Yogic life which has remained unquestionable and incontrovertible. It must also be borne in mind that this Yogic life is to be made continuous one without anticipating results but with steady mind and strong determination. Its objective is a long term affair and the aspirant should be prepared to be patient to pursue it whole heartedly and single-mindedly. Then the results are assured and follow naturally under no compulsions. Patañjali's *Yoga Sūtras* presents Yoga philosophy and technique in intelligible and rational way and an intelligent student can derive first its theoretical knowledge and only on deep conviction he can enter the path of practical Yoga and bring about fundamental changes in this nature and realize the ultimate goal.

The text gives the fundamental teachings of Yoga not from any angle or on the basis of any particular school of philosophy but the *Sādhaka* will see for himself that it is a Science of sciences and too comprehensive in its nature and too profound in its doctrines to be fitted into the framework of any particular philosophy. It stands in its own right as a science not based on the laws of material science but on the eternal laws of creation. It doesn't require any support from any philosophical school for its cognency, coherence, conviction, and clarity. It has its own truth, base knowledge and experience. Its truths are based on the experiences and experiments of an unbroken line of mystics, occultists, saints and sages who have realized and borne witness to them throughout the ages.

Chapter III

Buddhism grew out of reaction to the prevailing strong ritualistic Vedic tradition. Siddhārta, the founder, was born and brought up in Sanātana Dharma. He felt greatly disturbed by the poverty, sickness and death he saw. He was constantly haunted by the suffering in the world, and hence, he renounced his happy, luxurious palace life to seek answers. Dressed in monk's robes, he fasted and tortured his body. He was emaciated, but determined. As he neared death, he realized that if he died he would never find the answers he sought. So, he took food and water and vowed to continue his meditation even more deeply. As he sat under a *bodhi* tree he continued till the first rays of the sun brought inner light to him. He realized that all the suffering in the world comes from our own minds and our own actions. The way to live, he found, is not to engage in extremes but to follow with greater awareness along a middle path. Buddha's path is the Middle Way, neither engaging in extremes of self-indulgence nor self-denial.

Several centuries after the death of Buddha, the religion he had founded had split into four schools. Vaibhāṣika (direct realism), Santrāntika (indirect realism), Yogācārya (idealism) and Mādhyamika (relativism or nihilism). The first two philosophical schools belong to Hinayāna (the small vehicle which does not advocate worshipping the images of Buddha) and the last two to Mahāyāna (the great vehicle which believes in many incarnations of Buddha). Zen is connected with the Mādhyamika School, which was established by Nāgārjuna in the second century A.D.

But, the philosophy prefessed by Nāgārjuna was actually born one day when Buddha was speaking to a group of disciples at Vulture Peak. As Buddha ended his sermon he held a flower in his hands and looked out over the intent listeners. Only one disciple, Mahākaśyapa, smiled and he experienced an awakening communicated directly from Buddha. This was the first direct transmission, mind to mind, the cornerstone of Zen. Words and studies are secondary to Zen enlightenment. Mahākaśyapa became the second patriarch of Buddhism and was fundamental in carrying forth Buddha's teachings. He organized the first council of followers and appealed to them recall collectively the teachings and memorize them so, that his sermons would be remembered. These teachings, or *sūtras*, became the basis of Buddhism.

Buddhism traveled to China first and then to Korea and Japan in the first century A.D. For centuries Taoism and Confucianism had been intimately woven into the fabric of Chinese culture. Taoism is called the way of heaven, Confucianism the way of Man. Taoism emphasizes spirituality, Confucianism the ethical behaviour. The one represents the inner, the other the outer harmony. Mahāyāna Buddhism reached the Chinese soil during the first century A.D. China avidly embraced Buddhism and by 500 A.D. Buddhism was even more popular in China than it had been in India.

Chapter IV

The first patriarch of Zen was an Indian Buddhist monk who was given the name Bodhidharma by his teacher of Buddhism, Pranatara. It is said Bodhidharma went to China in 526 A.D. by crossing the Himālayas, Tibet and Gobi desert. He met Liang Wū-to, emperor of southern China, and interacted with him over the way. During the course of interaction, it is said, that Bodhidharma, in reply to several questions, said that merit derives from wisdom which is cultivated by meditation, not external acts, and to another question by the emperor "who is that replies to me?" he said, "I myself do not know who he is".[1] Bodhidharma's answers shocked and confused the emperor who could not understand the way preached by the former. Disillusioned, Bodhidharma traveled to a cave near the Shaolin temple in Hunam province and sat facing a wall, which was known as "wall-meditation" in which there is no view or scenery to look at. Today this sitting meditation known as ZaZen is practiced in China and Japan.

Zen masters are tough and severe. They do not easily bend to the seekers who are put to severe tests of discipline and sincerity. Only a serious and sincere seeker is received. According to one legend once a young monk by name Shen Kuang earnestly implored Bodhidharma to teach him the truth of Zen, but the Master was unbending. Every time when Shen approached Bodhidharma, the latter rejected. Shen never gave up his pursuits. One evening he waited for Bodhidharma in the thick snow storm which had almost buried him. The latter noticed him and asked, "What do you want me to do for you?" Shen replied: "I have come to receive your invaluable instruction. Pray, open your gate of mercy and extend your hand of salvation to this poor suffering mortal". On his imploring Bodhidharma replied: "the incomparable doctrine of Buddha can be comprehended only after a long, hard discipline and by enduring what is most difficult to endure, and by practicing what is most difficult to practice. Men of inferior virtue and wisdom cannot understand it. All the labours of such men will come to naught". To prove his sincerity Shen picked up a sword, cut off his left hand, and gave it to the Master. "I do not want your hand. Bring your soul here and I will pacify it", replied Bodhidharma. Shen hesitated for a moment and then said, "I have sought my soul for many years and I am still unable to get hold of it." "There", said Bodhi, "Your soul is pacified once and for all".[2] Shen became the second patriarch of Zen, carrying forth the spirit of Zen.

Another legend tells that Bodhidharma grew old and

wished to return to India. One day he called together all of his disciples and asked them: "Tell me, what have you learned from me?" The first disciple said, "According to me the truth is above affirmation and negation, for this is the way it moveth." The master said, "you have got my skin". Next a nun said: "As I understand it it is like Ānanda's viewing the Buddha land of Akṣobhaya. It is seen once and never again." The master said, "you have got my flesh". The third spoke: "Empty are the four elements (air, fire, water and earth) and non-existent the five *skandhas* (form, feeling, perception, impression and consciousness). According to my view, there is not a thing to be grasped as real". The master said, "you have got my bones". Finally, Shen Kuang, who had offered his hand to the master years before, reverentially stood and said nothing. Bodhidharma joyfully announced, "you have my marrow".

Zen was taught personally. Enlightenment was communicated directly from teacher to student, much like it was first taught by Buddha to Mahākaśyapa. This form of learning continues today. Zen wisdom is still communicated through contact between teacher and student and is called direct transmission.

Chapter V

The early Chinese patriarchs were well versed in the Chinese classics, and they integrated Zen with the accepted philosophies of China, particularly Taosim which sees all phenomenon in the world as yin and yang opposites. Buddhism views all as emptiness. Zen blends the two. The third patriarch, Sengts' an integrated both Buddhism and Taoism to form the unique synthesis. The fourth patriarch, Tao-Hsin (580-651), organized the first Zen community; here, monks lived separated from their families and society. Hung-Sen, the fifth patriarch, inspired many great Zen masters who founded sects of Zen that endured for several generations. Hui-Neng (638-713), the sixth patriarch, brought about a new emphasis. He was said to be a poor, illiterate firewood cutter. One day, just after having sold some of his firewood in the market place, he came upon a man reciting one of the most famous Mahāyāna sūtras, the Diamond Sūtra (Jewel of transcendental wisdom). Hui listened to the words and let a profound change take place. Unexpectedly and in a flash of sudden insight, he was enlightened. The idea that anyone, even a simple peddler, could become suddenly enlightened became one of the seminal ideas in Hui-Neng's Zen.

Hui journeyed to the temple of Hung, the fifth patriarch, to deepen his understanding. Monasteries usually excluded uneducated people, but Hui-Neng was accepted as a lay monk and given the job of pounding rice and splitting firewood. Hung-Jin recognized that his new student had natural talent.

Eventually, the fifth patriarch was ready to retire and appoint a successor. Hung asked his students to compose a poem that epitomized their insight. Shen-Hsin, the senior student, composed the following poem:

> Our body is the *bodhi* tree
> and our mind a mirror bright
> Carefully we wipe them now by hour
> And let no dust alight.[3]

On hearing this poem, Hui-Neng composed his own deeper poem:

> There is no *bodhi* tree
> nor stand of a mirror bright
> Since all is void
> where can the dust alight?[4]

The master listened to both poems and recognized Hui-Neng's wisdom. According to what was written in the Platform Sūtra, since Hung-Jin believed that his disciples would not accept an illiterate work as his successor, so, he secretly sent Hui-Neng off to the south to start his own school of Zen and Shen-Hsin to the north to found the Northern school. The latter taught that calm, quiet meditation gradually led practitioners to an enlightened life. But, the northern Zen, however, did not last long. By contrast, Hui-Neng's southern school was active, guiding students to sudden awakenings. He accepted students irrespective of their background because he firmly believed, based on his own experience, that "the essence of mind is already pure and free." Neither long study nor unusual talent was necessary to achieve enlightenment. Any one from a lowly class to a royal class can realize this simple truth. Hui-Neng's southern school became the dominant force. Most modern schools of Zen trace their roots back to Hui-Neng.

Hui-Neng's Zen spread throughout China freely. The Tang period (618-907) was one of the most creative and innovative for Zen in China. During this period, Zen masters found ways to teach without using rational explanations, often without words. The followers of Hui-Neng's Zen believed in the original nature of man which is pure, just as it is; the mind is already Buddha. Why try to cleanse it? However, Pai-Chang (720-814), one of the many great masters of this period, imposed rules for every day life in the Zen monastery. All monks must take vows to live an absolutely ethical life. They must do some form of work along with daily meditation. He believed that the Buddha mind should be able to penetrate into all aspects of life, including work. After all, Hui-Neng, the founder of this school, was a firewood cutter. One day, Pai-Chang's students, thinking they would give their master a rest from working in the field, hid his gardening tools. Pai refused to eat. Finally, the monks had no choice but to return his tools, Pai told them: "A day without work is a day without food". This became the motto for all the Zen monasteries that followed.

Zen's most creative masters lived and taught during the Tang dynasty, but more people practiced Zen than ever before during the Śuṅga dynasty (960-1279). Two major schools became dominant. Lin-Chi's Rinzai and Ts'ao-tung, later to be known as Soto in Japan. In order to accommodate the large number of students who wanted to learn Zen, the masters devised new ways to teach. One of the ways was creating enigmatic stories and riddles which came to be known as Kung-ans (Koans in Japanese). These were often paradoxically mysterious and puzzling. Conscious thinking cannot solve these koans. Only when conscious thinking is set aside enlightenment could happen with time. Koans were collected into two books, such as the *Mumonkan* (Gateless Gate) and the *Hekiganroku* (Blue Cliff Record).

Early Soto practitioners criticized this application of koan practice, claiming that it can wean away the students' attention from meditation, the true source of enlightenment. They drew from the original message of Bodhidharma and believed that sudden enlightenment was not the goal. It was better to practice daily meditation and faster or deep, continuous awareness, calm and clear.

Chapter VI

Zen spread to Korea directly from China before it went to Japan. Korea was introduced to Buddhism from China during the Three Kingdom period (37 BC - A.D. 668) of its history. Won-Hyo (617-686) popularized Buddhism in Korea. He wrote extensively on Buddhism. After enlightenment, he did not withdraw into a monastry. Instead, he spent his time helping the common people; after all these people needed help, not the virtuous. He believed enlightenment should be for every one, not just the elite. He taught how to meditate deeply to be happy and enlightened.

Koreans traveled to China and studied Zen under Matsu's students (Hui-Neng's Southern School) during the Tang dynasty period. Upon their return to Korea they founded Zen monasteries in the sparsely populated mountain regions. These monasteries became known as the Nine Mountain Schools, the foundational structure for Zen in Korea. Chinul (1158-1210) was recognized not only in Korea but also in China as one of Korea's greatest Zen monks. He taught that each individual has a sentient intelligence, the Buddha nature. This intelligence is what makes it possible for human beings to become enlightened. He expounded both gradual and sudden approaches to enlightenment. Sudden enlightenment happens in an instant of direct intense realization. But learning does not stop with the first light of insight. Gradually, the student depends it to experience truer understanding at the absolute level of wisdom. His teachings were specific and detailed, offering techniques to the students of varied intellectual and spiritual capacity. He believed in the use of intellect to check the negative habits. As he explained to his students; "Hence sudden and gradual cultivation are like the two wheels of a cart: neither one can be missing".[5]

Chinul introduced a new tool of meditation called hwadu, shorter than Koans. Here students were instructed to focus attention on the hwadu as a kind of Yogic concentration to block out distractions and interpretations and thus achieve a deep focus on the essence of Koan. The discursive intellect was by passed. Chinul felt that this method was a direct path to enlightenment. He offered a unified group to promote unity among different schools.

Chapter VII

Buddhism was introduced in Japan in 552 A.D. It soon grew to be a well-established institution. It has attracted royal support and patronage for hundreds of years. Zen was brought to Japan between A.D. 600 and A.D. 800, but it did not take hold until a dedicated Buddhist monk named Myoan Eisai (1141-1215) founded a Zen temple that endured. But he made a pilgrimage to China to deepen his knowledge and revitalize Buddhism in Japan. Upon his return to Japan, he founded a new line of Tendai called Yojo (Shingon and Tendai were the two prominent sects of Buddhism in Japan before Zen was introduced). Not satisfied, he returned to China to retrace Buddhism to its roots in India. But he was unsuccessful, so he did the next best thing and studied Zen in China and returned to Japan to revitalize Japanese Buddhism. Despite resistance from Tendai and Shingon sects, he established a temple in 1202 in Kyoto which became an important centre for Zen. He was credited for not only bringing Zen to Japan but also introducing tea. Although Eisai's Zen was always mixed with Tendai, he had planted the seeds. His students carried on the Rinzai Zen traditions that Eisai had started, firmly rooting Zen in Japan.

DoZen (1200-1253) was a young student of MyoZen, one of Eisai's students. He too, in order to deepen his understanding and reform Buddhism in Japan, undertook a journey to China. There he met Ju-Ching (1163-1228) who was considered to be a master of pure Zen. As a follower of the T'sao-tung tradition (Soto Zen), Ju-Ching was against Rinzai's use of Koans and its emphasis on sudden enlightenment. DoZen learnt from him that practice is not separate from enlightenment. Enlightenment and practice are one. Upon his return to Japan, he established Soto Zen tradition above politics and cities and influences and exhorted his students to give up all attachments and live a simple life devoted to concentrated meditation, which he called ZaZen (sitting meditation). His institutions for ZaZen were simple: Find a quiet place, sit on a pillow in a cross-legged position, with body straight, upright and two thumbs together at the tips. Keep your breathing steady, while forgetting all attachments. If a wish arises, take note of it and then let it go. DoZen broke ties with Tendai and Shingon and taught pure Zen and only Zen. Nothing was necessary other than sitting in meditation. He taught that practice is enlightenment. DoZen explained: we do not practice to become enlightened, we practice as a natural expression of our enlightenment.

Many Chinese masters, from more than twenty lines of Zen, migrated to Japan, helping the Zen movement to grow. Both Soto and Rinzai Zen flourished and spread. Rinzai tended to be located in the cities, while Soto Temples spread throughout the rural areas. Soto practitioners emphasized ZoZen as the central practice. They were opposed to Rinzai practitioners who emphasized koans along with other practices. Fierce rivalry existed between them.

Chapter VIII

The foregone cursory glance at the developments in Buddhism testifies how the original teachings of Buddha had been changed and modified to suit not so much the needs of times but the conflicting individual egos that emerged from time to time in China, Korea, Japan and other south-east Asian countries. Now, we shall examine the similarities and differences between Zen and Yoga. As for the commonalities, **first,** both were ancient and originated in India. **Second**, both are optimistic philosophies and not religions which firmly believe that all people have the capacity for enlightenment latent within. This potential often becomes actualized suddenly in Zen while in Yoga it is gradual. Yoga philosophy was a systemized philosophical tradition. Until Patañjali's times it was practiced in umpteen ways. It was Patañjali who had organized it in a systematic way. **Three,** both Yoga and Buddhism were shorn of rituals. Buddha protested against the rituals being over practiced in Indian society during his times. He felt how the real core of Upaniṣads had been subverted and surpassed by the excess rituals that came later and were promoted by Brahminical castes. Let us not forget the fact that the pure wisdom found in the Upaniṣads was free from all rituals. Buddha in his search for the meaning and purpose of life touched this core whatever the arguments might be.

Four, Buddhism became Zen when it traveled to the far east. Zen is the Japanese pronunciation of the Chinese word *Chan-na* which is the corrupt form of Sanskrit word *dhyāna* or the *Pāli* word *jhana*. Zen Buddhism is remarkably simplified form of Buddhism. It is not a religion, but a way to enlightenment. It originated in India but was systematized and developed in China before it was transmitted to Korea and Japan. Similarly, Yoga is not a religion, nor a philosophy but a way of life, a way to *Kaivalya*.

Five, both Yoga and Zen aim at realizing enlightenment. In Yoga system Patañjali uses the bigger 'Self' which is no different from Buddhahood, the Pure Consciousness. **Six,** both Yoga and Buddhism are chiefly concerned about the correction of mind which is the root cause of all suffering and working and pain in the world. Patañjali identifies modifications (*vṛttis*) as the cause for suffering. As long as the *vṛttis* are present experiencing the Ultimate is impossible. Stilling the mind is the paramount condition for experiencing this state. The entire Yoga philosophy is aimed at eliminating the *vṛttis* so that a state of mind is created which becomes the starting point for the real spiritual odyssey. Patañjali prescribes the eight fold path (*Āṣṭāṅga Yoga*) to attain this state. Buddha on the other uses 'desire' (*tṛṣṇā*) for 'modification' and identifies it as the cause of suffering (*duḥkha*) in the world. He too presents eight fold path which is moralistic and ethical. He believes that unless a clear cut ethical discipline is followed, which can check the modifications; it becomes impossible for the individual to tread the higher path of spirituality which leads to *Kaivalya* or *Nirvāṇa*. Patañjali prescribes in the form of five *Yamas* and five *Niyamas* at the lower level as the starting point for higher spiritual life which in his *Āṣṭāṅga Yoga* constitutes *dhāraṇa, dhyāna* and *samādhi*. The Buddhist rules of conduct and discipline for living an ethical life were absolutely essential to DoZen; the founder of Soto School. Disciples should accept and commit themselves to living according to compassionate and selfless guidelines. Following the ethical discipline helps disciples orient themselves correctly towards themselves and others, opening the door to a meditative life. As DoZen said, "How can you expect to become a Buddha if you do not guard against faults and prevent yourself from doing wrong".[6] All of the Zen monks who studied with DoZen swore to uphold the Buddhist precepts, and this continues to be an important part of all traditional Zen practice today.

Zen consists of puzzling language, baffling attitudes and surprising methods. It exists in and of itself. True Zen is in every living thing. It is consciousness in action. More than any limited awareness, it opens every inner door to our infinite nature. Instantly the mind becomes free. Yoga too aims at unearthing this pure consciousness that lies underneath mind which does not have any existence apart from *vṛttis* (modifications). Until these *vṛttis* are eliminated the individual cannot discover his true nature. All Yoga is aimed at eliminating these *vṛttis*. Patañjali lays down the ethical and moral discipline for the *sādhaka* in order to make himself fitting vehicle for the higher state. **Seven,** *Dhyāna* is the key word both in Yoga and Zen. *Dhyāna* is impossible as long as *vṛttis* act upon the *sādhaka*. The object of it is to discover the true nature of being. The word *samādhi* used in Yoga system is not to be confused with the state of Buddhahood in Zen. *Samādhi* is a combination of two Sanskrit words, '*Sama*' meaning balance and '*ādhi*' meaning in the beginning, which reveals that in the beginning everything is in perfect balance, calm and quiet. Consciousness is ever pure, calm and quiet. This is the true nature of whole existence but, the question is how to attain this state? This state is not lost; it is there. Zen preaches that it is never lost, it is ever present. Realizing this is enlightenment. But, right now, in all human beings it is temporarily clouded with *vṛttis*. These *vṛttis, saṁskāras* and *vāsanās* have to be unshackled to attain the state of pure consciousness. For which practice (*sādhana*) is a must as sudden realization is impossible in all cases. This practice ultimately leads to realization. But, a note of caution here. Both practice and realization are not two separate things. The one implies the other. The practice is realization. This principle is found both in Yoga and Zen.

Eight, there are two aspects both in Yoga and Zen,

inwardly and outwardly. Inwardly, both are an experience, a realization, a state of enlightenment. Outwardly, both stand as a tradition and a way of living. But unlike Yoga teachers, Zen teachers are very puzzling. They present their students with dilemmas in order to teach them to teach themselves. Zen koans are dilemmas, or enigmas, that teachers give to their students. A koan is a riddle without a logical answer. Its purpose is to help the mind break free from logic. It is important to notice that Koans are only the highlights of the play, not the complete drama. Placing too much attention on solving Koans nullifies the idea of abrupt enlightenment.

Nine, the relationship between the guru and the disciple is very important in the Zen tradition as in the Upaniṣadic tradition. But the role of guru is minimal and marginal in both the tradition. He is only a pointer or a helper. He shows the way, ultimately it is the individual who has to work out his own salvation. In both the traditions, one should obey the instructions of his guru implicitly and work hard for enlightenment. There is a saying in the Zen tradition. Before illumination, one chops wood and carries water and after illumination, one chops wood and carries water. Inner life changes but outer life remains the same.

Ten, mindfulness is an important teaching in Zen. It is true mind that is like a mad monkey, difficult to be controlled, but Patañjali says that one can control the mind by twin virtues, *abhyāsa* (practice) and *vairāgya* (detachment).

Practice is knowledge cum action. It is systematic, repeated performance involving a certain methodology to accomplish higher proficiency. While detachment is knowledge cum devotion to the higher. "If practice is the path of evolution, renunciation is the path of involution"[7] says B.K.S. Iyengar, an authoritarian on Haṭha Yoga. The two have to be balanced for a harmonious development. In the *Āṣṭāṅga Yoga*, the first five limbs represent the evolutive path and the remaining three the involutive path. Both *abhyāsa* and *vairāgya* must go hand in hand Patañjali insists; and one cannot ascend to spiritual heights without the other.

As *vṛttis* can be controlled through these twin virtues in Yoga, so in the Zen tradition ZaZen practice stops the waves of the mind gradually. Zen admits the presence of these waves as necessary and the practitioner should not worry too much about them and he should not take them in negative sense. Zen speaks the presence of such waves will eventually enrich the practice and the practice in which such waves should be ignored will help him make remarkable progress. Thus, both in Yoga and Zen constant practice is insisted upon. It is said in Zen tradition: "It is impossible, however, to attain absolute calmness of our mind without any effort. We must make some effort, but we must forget ourselves in the effort we make. In this realm there is no subjectivity or objectivity. Our mind is just calm, without even any awareness. In this unawareness, every effort and every idea and thought will vanish."[8]

Chapter IX

As for the differences, **first,** realization in Yoga is not sudden but gradual and evolutionary. Whereas Zen schools profess both sudden and gradual enlightenment. **Two,** the ethical discipline in Yoga is prescriptive and determined. Patañjali prescribes five principles in Yama (*Ahiṁsā-satyāsteya-brahmacarya parigraha yamaḥ–Sādhana Pāda; sūtra 30)* and five in Niyama (*śauca-santōṣa-tapas-svadhyāyēśvara-pranidhanāṁ niyamaḥ–Sādhana Pāda; sūtra : 32).* In Zen too the ethical position is fundamental but unlike Patañjali the Zen Masters say it is implicit in the standpoint of emptiness and unity. Zen draws its ethical perspective from Mahāyāna Buddhist philosophy, which believes objective reality is not a distinct, unchallengeable certainty. Nothing exists and yet all things exist simultaneously is the governing principle. Zen Buddhists do not distinguish between the individual self and the external world in the ultimate sense. We are not separate or separable from the world. We are part of it. Practice and enlightenment are one and not separate from each other. They believe that actions are not reciprocal.

Reciprocity is not required because we cannot separate ourselves from the other, our actions, or their consequences. Actions are performed for their own sake, not because of outside pressure. D.T. Suzuki refers to this as secret virtue. "Secret virtue is the deed done for its own sake, not looking for any form of compensation anywhere, neither in heaven nor on earth"[9], Good behaviour flows from giving oneself fully to the needs of the situation.

Zen does not prescribe in its doctrine what actions to take moment to moment. But Hui-Neng, the Sixth Patriarch, encouraged the monks to take refuge in precepts he called "the three gems of our essence of mind". These three gems are three vows: *buddha*, which stands for enlightenment; *dharma*, which stands for orthodoxy; *saṅgha* (the order), which stands for purity. He explained that when people take refuge in enlightenment, evil impulses and ideas do not use. Taking refuge in the *dharma* keeps people free from cravings, egotism, and arrogance. Refuge in purity implies that people will not be drawn to the many temptations in this outer world. The nature of these primary precepts however does not prescribe how to act or what to do. Rather, the vows are an absolute commitment to enlightenment. From the absolute standpoint of enlightenment, ethical action flows naturally, Zen asserts.

The quintessence of Zen is "Look into the mind and you will find Buddhahood". As the story goes, DoZen (1200-1253), the founder of ZoZen (sitting meditation) asked his teacher, "if by nature everybody is Buddha, then why do they practice meditation?" No one could answer his question. So, he went to China and after experiencing the truth, he returned to Japan and started his own, the Soto School, which teaches that if the means are perfect, the end becomes perfect. That is the main focus of Zen Buddhism. DoZen's motto is "Practice and realization are not different. Practice is a matter of realization. It is taught that practice is to be done with care, but we are never to look for some realization apart from the practice, for practice is merely directing attention to the original realization".[10]

Three, in Zen there is no concentration but only meditation while in Yoga Patañjali assigns an important position to concentration (*dhāraṇa*), which is a step to *dhyāna*. Patañjali says *dhāraṇa* prepares the *sādhaka* for *dhyāna*. For, according to him, *dhāraṇa* focuses the mind on a particular object fully; thereby, it achieves the understanding of the essential nature of the object itself leading to a greater transformation in consciousness. Only when the practitioner masters it or makes considerable progress, he can enter into *dhyāna*. To achieve this state Patañjali prescribes the first five stages at the lower level *yama, niyama, āsana, prāṇāyāma* and *pratyahāra* as these steps would check and eliminate mental and physical distractions and prepare the *sādhaka* for the higher Yoga which consists of *dhāraṇa, dhyāna* and *samādhi*. When the body-mind complex is freed from all kinds of distractions, the *sādhaka* can focus his mind on a particular object leading to *dhāraṇa*. Patañjali stipulates the practice of the lower limbs, without which the *sādhaka* though may bypass and move straight to *dhyāna* and succeed initially, may not fully achieve progress. Hence, Patañjali insists on purification as a necessary condition for the higher Yoga.

In Zen such elaborate process is not proposed. Zen primarily deals with meditation. It is the cornerstone in Zen. In fact the root meaning of Zen is meditation. The Japanese word Zen translates as 'meditation'. All sects of Zen practice meditation even though they may vary on customs, traditions, and other aspects of Zen life. Meditation is the means to experience Zen for yourself. Dozen believed that ZaZen was the "right entrance to the Buddha Dharma". Since meditative practice itself is enlightenment, there is nothing outside the mind to seek, and nothing outside meditation to do. Zen believes the mind is the crux of a living man. Mind is everything and nothing. Hence, if this is subdued and sublimated, greater awareness is created, that is the essence of man's being. This is the pivotal teaching of Zen tradition. Further, Zen has given seven ways to practice in meditation. These seven ways are practiced in different schools within the tradition. Patañjali does not discuss such steps. He however, expounds different techniques in *dhāraṇa*. The seven ways to meditation in Zen include: the first is through breathing exercises. The technique is simple. Sit on a cushion on the floor with legs crossed and hands rested comfortably in the lap or draped over the knees. Close eyes and turn attention to breathing. Pay attention to the air as it moves into the nose and goes down into the lungs. Notice how the chest expands and lifts naturally as the air moves down, then drops slightly as the air moves out. Do not try to force or alter breathing in any way. Keep bringing attention back to breathing if it wanders away. As you become more adept, you will be able to stay with this for longer periods of time. In this meditation one can begin to experience Oneness with meditation. If you can allow natural, uninhabited breathing with full attention, you will begin to catch a glimpse of the Zen mind. The second way is by concentrating on one point. The third way is through visualization. The fourth way is through a mantra. One of the popular Buddhist mantras is "*Oṁ maṇi pạdme huṃ*". The fifth is with movement, which was invented by Taoist Yogi, San Fing Chang of the Ming Dynasty in China. The sixth way is by absorbing one's mind in unlimited goodwill or devotional thoughts. There are four unlimited thoughts in Zen Buddhism: *Maitrī* (friendliness), *karuṇā* (compassion), *mudita* (sympathetic joy) and *upekṣā* (even mindedness). The last method is by identifying the mind essence. This is the effortless meditation of Zen meditation without anything on which to meditate. J. Krishnamurti talks a great deal about this sort of meditation in his teachings..

The sole aim of Zen is to enable oneself to understand, realize, and ultimately perfect ones own mind. The mind is the keystone of Zen studies. The essence of mind is illuminated void. The Buddhist teaching of vividness is comprehensive and profound. There is a Zen story about the mind. Once a flying angel discovered the fully illuminated forest. He descended and found Boddhisattva in deep meditation. The angel in curiosity awakened the Boddhisattva and asked. "Sir, I did not see into your mind. Could you tell me what the object of your meditation is"? Buddhisattva only smiled.[11]

Four, Emptiness is fundamental to Zen. The stories, customs and traditions are like a handicrafted box; their usefulness is in their emptiness. One of the principles on which Zen is based is: "Form is emptiness, emptiness is form". The concept of 'nothing' was a unique discovery of the Hindus. The Hindus were the first to recognize zero, which they called *śūnyạ*, meaning void or empty. Mathematics became possible from this zero by computing this as "something". Mạhāyāna Buddhism's emptiness, known as *śūnyata*, was the spring board for Zen. In Zen, emptiness is not a concept or goal, nor is it an ultimate state. It is a process, a continuum, always in flux. This is different from the western scientific concept that defines emptiness as a state, a vacuum consisting of the absence of molecules.

Zen masters however discourage immersion in any kind of empty state. They urge students not to get stuck in the swamp of nothingness. A story is related to this. Once when Yamaooka Teshu (1836-1888) was a young Zen student, he searched for enlightenment by visiting one Zen master after another. In his search, he met Master Dokuon of Shokoku and talked about the nature of all things as emptiness. Dokuon watched him silently, and later he lifted his bamboo stick and struck Tesshu who felt himself fill with anger. Then Dokuon said, "If nothing exists, where did that anger come from?"[12] Instead of trying to make yourself nothing, make nothing your true self– this is the philosophy of Zen.

The concept of emptiness further needs a greater understanding and clarification in the light of Vedāntic concept of Self which is reinstated with great vigour and conviction in Patañjali's Yoga. According to Buddhist thinking, the idea that we have a separate self is an illusion. There is no external individual being apart from interaction with the world. Each of us has individual perceptions, consciousness, and sensations. All of us pass through these experiences. Yet to gather all of these experiences into a fixed concept of a 'self' is a mistake. This is a false inference. Patañjali dismisses this petty 'self' as something existent and real. Experiencing takes place. Nothing more. Nothing can be drawn from this. Rene Descartes's famous conclusion does not necessarily follow. Instead of his statement "I think, therefore I am", Zen Buddhists say "I think I am, therefore I appear". In Descartes's statement "I am" affirms the existence of 'self' which is non-existent, does not have any identity of its own existence apart from its relation to the external world. Zen Buddhists however hold the view that individual 'self' is actually an expression of the true Self, which is deeply spiritual and one with all things.

If the concept of 'self' is an illusion, then so too is the concept of the other; 'no-self' in Zen also means 'no-other'.

If 'mine' is an illusion, the 'other' too is an illusion. There is no 'self', there is 'no other'– all disappear in the Oneness. When Emperor Wu asked Bodhidharma, "who is this standing before me"? and Bodhidharma answered, "I do not know".[13] He really did not know.

Patañjali explains the 'self' in a different manner. He identifies the three aspects corresponding to the subjective and objective sides of manifestation as knower, knowing and the known or cognizer, cognition and cognized or perceiver, perception and perceived. Patañjali says that the One (the Ultimate Reality being Pure Consciousness) has become the three which causes confusion and false identity. It is because the one reality has become the three, Patanjali says, that it is possible to bring about a fusion of the three into one, and it is this kind of fusion which is the essential technique of *Samādhi*.

Patañjali considers factors preventing this process of assimilation. First, the various tendencies, some almost instinctive in character, for example, those of accumulating possessions, indulging in all kinds of enjoyments, attractions and repulsions are derived from desires tend to throw up the mind out of gear. All such tendencies may be eliminated through the practice of *Yama, Niyama* and *Vairāgya*. Then come the sensuous impressions derived from the contact of the sense-organs with the external world. These impressions can be cut off by means of *Āsana, Prāṇāyāma* and *Pratyahāra*. Now, the Yogi has to deal with the inherent activity of the mind itself, which can be controlled and canalized by *Dhāraṇa* and *Dhyāna*.

Five, another difference between Yoga and Zen is that the latter epitomizes self awakening beyond words. Direct, non-conceptual experience goes straight to one core rather than interpretative analysis. Yet Zen attests to the fact that words and concepts do have a place. Although Zen masters often seem to derogate words, properly used words and concepts are a valuable tool in Zen. Zen masters guide students indirectly through action, stories, and even silence. It told many meaningful, colourful, thought provoking stories to their students. Rinzai Zen developed the Koan system to help students find and develop the awakened awareness that is called enlightenment. Even Soto Zen, with its emphasis on ZaZen meditation, draws from stories of Zen masters. D.T. Suzuki, explains the importance of Koans ".. When the koans are understood, the master's state of mind is understood, which is *satori* and without which Zen is a sealed book".[14]

A koan is not a conundrum or a riddle to be solved by a nimble wit. It is not a verbal psychiatric device. Explanations are not given. Instead, students are asked to meditate on the story carefully without analyzing or reverting to rational thinking. The story itself offers an opportunity for experience beyond the usual words. Ruth Fuller Saraki, one of the first western women to become involved in Zen in America, explained, "when the koan is resolved it is realized to be a simple and clear statement made from the state of consciousness which it has helped to awaken".[15]

Chinese Zen masters Ma-tsu and Lin-chi often resorted to shouting or hitting in response to student's questions. The purpose was not to terrorize the students but to give them a direct wordless, non-conceptual experience. Frequently, students who were struck by Lin-Chi's stick discovered sudden enlightenment. Here is a typical exchange between Lin-Chi and a student.

> The Master said to a man,
> "well come, or ill come?"
> The man gave a shout.
> The master picked up his stick and said,
> "speak then, speak!"
> The nun shouted once more
> The Master struck her.[16]

Like any teaching device, koans, shouting, and strikes with the stick are not the awareness itself. They are aids to engage students toward awakening.

There are several paths to Zen awakening propounded by different sects of Zen. Although all Zen Buddhists accept that mind is the Buddha, there are differences in how to realize this. Rinzai practitioner believes in the use of koan that would destroy the barriers. Students are given a koan when they first enter the monastery and are told to work on it. Each day they see the teacher for a short session, called Dokusan. As soon as the student masters one koan, a new one is given. Rinzai schools present five levels of Koans.

After the fifth level, (Mu) some schools such as Zen mountain monastery in New York present students with the precepts, the moral and ethical teachings of Buddha, treating them like a koan. Students meditate on the precepts to learn how to truly live enlightenment acting ethically each moment.

Soto Zen on the other hand believes in ZaZen only (*Shikantaza*). Koans are a means of focusing attention while sitting in meditation. Sitting need not mean really sitting down. Standing, walking, and working are not different in entering the way. Meditation and work are the main stays of life at Soto Zen monasteries, with little use of Koans.

Zen believes in deep, clear awareness that opens a new vista of experience, transferring the person. As Bodhidharma said, "the opening of the inner eye is the door of the Great Vehicle".[17] Every thing is different and yet nothing is different. This is the paradox of enlightenment.

Six, Zen and Yoga also differ in the matter of acquiring extraordinary powers (*siddhis*). Zen masters do not discuss these powers. They give least importance to these powers. They are more interested in self-awakening beyond words and concepts – how to quieten the mind so as to experience the One. Patañjali on the other devotes one section exclusively to *siddhis* (*Vibhūti Pāda, Sūtras* : 16 to 56) acquired through the practice of *saṁyama* (the fusion of *dhāraṇa, dhyāna* and *samādhi*). But these *siddhis* cannot be understood in the strict sense of 'powers'. The real meaning is best expressed by the word "accomplishments" connected with the attainment of the highest states of consciousness. Only in this sense, Patañjali says, the *siddhis* must be understood. It is no doubt that the advanced Yogi acquires these powers. But, if these are exhibited for the satisfaction of petty vanities or for earning money and fame, then, the purpose of Yoga is defeated. The unfoldment of Pure Consciousness alone matters in Yogic philosophy and nothing else. The *sādhaka* has to work only in this direction.

The best way to understand this aspect is to consider knowledge and power as two aspects of the same reality. So, every one who has the knowledge with regard to the inner working of any set of phenomena has also the power to manipulate phenomena. Both science and Yoga work on this assumption. But science has knowledge of only physical forces and can therefore control only physical phenomena. Yoga acquires knowledge of the far subtler and powerful forces of mind and consciousness and can, therefore, exercise powers connected with those inner forces. It is however not the intention of Patañjali to give a clear cut technique for the development of the *siddhis*. He merely gives a hint in each *sūtra* in the *Vibhūti Pāda* of the mental process whereby the particular result can be attained. The *sādhaka* must understand this particular point that underlies the *siddhis*. The main emphasis should be on finding the ultimate truth through self-realization and the *siddhis* should be used merely as a means for gaining that end.

Chapter X

Both Yoga and Zen lend themselves to psychotherapy in many ways. Both guide directly to the path of self-discovery. Both aim at using the mental illness. Zen, however, is limited as its methods and techniques are more directed to the controlling and emptying mind. It believes that if mind is taken care of, everything else in human life is in order. Yoga, on the other, in its and through *Āṣṭāṅga Yoga*, is methodical and systematic; and it appears that it is more holistic than Zen as it takes care of every aspect of human being the physical, the vital, the mental, the psychic and spiritual. In its discipline it appears to be more vigorous, arduous and severe than that of Zen. It helps the individual develop both physical and mental flexibility. Zen concentrates on mind and teaches us how to develop and expand our awareness.

Both Zen and Yoga consider the relative and absolute as two complementary levels of perspective. Each of us is unique and different from the other in the body-mind complex make-up. However, we are part of the Unknowable

Oneness. We have a self, yet we do not. Relative and absolute levels of relationship complement each other. Each depends on the other. Both are needed and neither is sufficient without the other. Both Zen and Yoga teach us that we should not be caught up too much in self-analysis, in false concerns which are only on the relative level.

The true self is 'no-self'. At the highest level it is neither self nor no-self. As *Samādhi* takes place, one experiences this state, and thereafter he lives constantly in this state. According to Zen philosophy, the true self is at one with the universe. There is no gap, no separation between ourselves and others. There is no outside. Nothing could be obtained. As Lin-chi said, "outside there is no *dharma*; inside there is none to be obtained".[18] It is simply wholeheartedness that can be directed to many activities of life. It is fully accepting oneself, here and now; it is here one discovers ones time self. Then one can experience what Lin-chi meant, when he said, "nothing is missing".

Unlike Yoga which is purely concerned with attaining *kaivalya* through purification of body and mind Zen has entered the arts and every aspect of life. An inseparable affinity has been developed between Zen and arts. A Zen practitioner can at best enter the artistic skills and make them fully perfect, flawless, and precision–like. Entering into art is a viable path way to experience enlightenment. As D.T. Suzuki said, "Art is studied in Japan not only for art's sake, but for spiritual enlightenment".[19]

Many different kinds of Zen art are practiced today.

Some of the best known are Cha-no-yu (the art of tea), calligraphy, Haiku (poetry), and martial arts. There are also the Zen arts of gardening Koto (incense), Sumi-e (ink painting), Kyudo (archery), Noh drama, Ikebana (flower arrangement), and Bonsai (miniature trees). Another area that has been influenced by Zen is psychotherapy. Several contemporary Zen masters are also psychotherapists. What is more noticeable in all these arts is precision with which artistic skill is executed. This requires an absolutely focused mind, at one with movement. This is achieved through meditation, through transformation and not with much thinking.

Zen arts epitomize the relationship between form and emptiness. The Heart Sūtra tells us that form is emptiness and emptiness is form – a central theme in Zen. Zen believes that it is only out of form that emptiness becomes possible. We do not strive to delete all thoughts to make mind empty. Rather we discover the emptiness that is already present within the form of thoughts, experiences, and realities. Each type of Zen art works with form in its own way to bring about the experience of emptiness. In painting and calligraphy, empty space is as important as lines. Haiku sparingly uses evocative words, linked to symbolic meanings to express emptiness. In Noh Drama, the void is expressed as movement just opposed against non-movement, rhythms to non-rhythms, chorus followed by silence. This has affected the modern theatre in the west.

Zen arts also differ from other forms of art in that they

are goalless. Zen artists approach their subject without a preconceived thought or plan of what it should be. In the process of creating the artist is lost in the artistic moment. Then the creation springs from its own true nature. The artist does not contemplate on what is being created. It simply happens, in a most neutral and spontaneous way. In the process the artist experiences the Oneness during brief moments. Zen artists immerse themselves fully in their art. They are selfless and purposeless and goalless. Their art flows out of the unity between the artist and the work, creator and creation, subject and object.

Art is simply art when it is taken along the Zen path of creation. It can apply to the whole life. In fact, the whole life is transformed into an art–living is an art. It can be of anything in life. Meditate before or during the work, and the awareness becomes deeper and deeper. It is from this deeper awareness springs the life of work. This is the most naturalistic way of doing things in life. This is the secret of Zen.

Zen is made explicitly affecting all aspects of human life. Its presence is seen and felt in arts. Thus art and Zen have become inseparable. That art is made possible in a more creative way is the seminal principle derived from Zen. Yoga too is a universal culture. It itself is an art, an art of all arts, the fundamental art as it encompasses the wholeness of a man. It is an art of the "inner".

The art of Yoga deals with living. Living is an art. The art of living is a great art – greater than all other arts because each performing art or fine art deals with one aspect of human creation. Hence, they are segmentary. Whereas the art of living is total, comprehensive and inclusive of everything else. It is not momentary, but moving from one moment to another with complete and total awareness. Hence, Yoga is the fundamental art. It deals with the art of living in its totality and not fragments. Hence, a Yogi is a greater artist than all other artists. His living itself is more creative, though he doesn't create like other artists. He makes his life more creative, dynamic, thrilling and exciting. He enjoys, unlike the other artists, every moment of life.

While other art forms are directed to the objective world, Yoga is purely concerned with the subjective world. There is no objective world without the subject. Everything is subjective, Yoga proceeds from the subject – the self. It helps man understand his own complex self. Understanding one's own self is not an easy task. It requires tremendous will power, courage and constant awareness. It does not involve segmentary understanding. It is total comprehension of the self– its mechanism, its intricacies, its nuances. A Yogi constantly makes an effort, and his effort is *sādhana* and this *sādhana* is a whole lifetime process. Sri Aurobindo thus calls "all life is Yoga". It includes all life on the earth. Therefore, all Yoga is art. Whereas other artists act in inspiration, transport themselves into a world of their own and create. But, soon, as the process of creation is over, they plummet into their own petty self. Therefore, an artist is an artist so long as he creates, while a Yogi is an artist for the whole of his life.

Yoga deals with man-making. It is the building of a whole man. Yoga is not mere postures and breathing. Nor is it a mere handbook of instructions as to how to live in a jungle, in a world negating retirement. It is not an impractical idealism – nor a dreamy ideology. But it deals with achieving equanimity, composure and ease at all times, and thus most effectively come to meet always his own personal, social and national problems. It tells us how man can live a better life in the world, and how he can gain a mastery over his destiny. Yoga is a great science, and it has a glorious utility in the world. It is not concerned with rituals and ceremonies, but it helps one discover in oneself a new strength and vitality to face one's own challenges in life, and provides a new world of inward courage of conviction to live honestly serving others. It deals with the wholeness of man. It shapes and moulds the whole being. It transforms man from his crude, despicable, diabolical form into a fine human being who can live with greater integrity, honesty, simplicity and truthfulness in the world. Such a man can easily influence his fellow beings and affect the society in a positive way. He can govern himself in the best possible way and he who governs himself needs no governance from outside. Good governance comes from within and that will remain steadfast and everlasting. That which comes from within has tremendous moral force and conviction and hence, it can never be crazed so early by outward forces. A Yogi needs no governance of whatsoever from outside, he leads a happy life. He who relies on governance from outside for his moral conduct will always suffer in conflicts. Yoga offers good governance of one self.

Yoga is also distinguished from the other arts in another dimension. Generally, art is an expression of the inner – the inner being, the emotional upheavals that happen to us in our day-to-day life. An artist uses these emotions and transforms them into artistic expression. Whereas a Yogi works to conquer them and cultivates empathy, compassion, friendliness, joy and indifference towards happiness and sorrow and service in order to achieve complete harmony with the cosmos. Yoga is a perfect art of the rhythmical movement of the inner. Though it doesn't express itself in any artistic form its dynamism is visible, and felt in every moment of living. Finally, he tries to realize *satyaṁ, śivaṁ* and *sundaraṃ* and lives in it. Thus, he divinizes his life. Whereas an art, though gives us aesthetic pleasure which is beyond sensual pleasure, still suffers from the lack of sublime which is divine. Yoga doesn't suffer from the lower. It aims at the higher life. The purpose of Yoga is to divinize life.

Such a man-making art is essential for social reconstruction. Any social reconstruction or reformation should start from the individual, who is a basic unit of society. Or any social reconstruction with structural changes in human institutions becomes incomplete unless and until it is accompanied by individual reconstruction. Yoga offers this reconstruction at the individual level. Yoga is firstly for individual growth, but through individual growth, society and community develop. It offers a solution to all problems of humanity. It brings a total change in life so that as individuals with a greater stability of mind we may achieve a greater harmony in our personal life, thereby in social life too. Individual growth is a must, if society needs growth in real life sense and Yoga develops each individual, if followed by letter and spirit.

Yoga is an integral art. It can be dealt from ethical, physical, psychological and spiritual levels. From the point of view of physical, Yoga removes toxins from the system and improves its health. From the psychological point of view, it quietens the mind. From the spiritual point of view, it takes the individual beyond mind and merges with the Cosmic. All the eight limbs of Yoga are made into ethical, physical, psychological and spiritual. These are gradual steps leading one to the other, finally to a greater spiritual height. Ethical Yoga comprises *Yama* and *Niyama*. These two are like the roots and the trunk of the tree. *Yama* principles include *ahiṁsā* (non-violence), *satya* (truthfulness), *āsteya* (freedom from avarice), *brahmacarya* (control of sensual pleasures) and *aparigraha* (non-covetousness) and *Niyama* principles comprise *śauca* (cleanliness), *santōṣa* (contentment), *tapas* (austerity), *svādhyāya* (self-study) and *Īśvara-Prāṇidhāna* (surrender through devotion). The physical Yoga comprises *Āsanas* and *Prāṇāyāma*. *Āsana* is the art of positioning the body which has two aspects, posing and reposing. Both have to be balanced to achieve good results in the body. Ultimately, *Āsanas* create a healthy body which is essential for mind to concentrate and meditate. The leaves are the *Prāṇāyāma*. As the leaves create the tree and provide nourishment for its healthy growth, so *Prāṇāyāma* feeds and aerates the cells, nerves, organs, intelligence and consciousness of the human system. Psychological Yoga includes *Pratyahāra* and *Dhāraṇa*. The bark is *Pratyahāra* translated as withdrawl of senses. The sap of the tree is *Dhāraṇa*, that is, concentration or complete attention which flows within the branches and the trunk of the tree towards the root. The spiritual Yoga comprises *Dhyāna* and *Samādhi*. The flower of the tree is *Dhyāna*, meditation, which balances the body, mind and intellect. And the last of the tree is fruit, which is *Samādhi*, wherein the ego is completely subdued and eliminated and a final merger with the Cosmic Consciousness takes place. In this state there is neither subject nor object. Everything gets dissolved. Thus, the tree of Yoga is an integral Yoga – *Yoga Vṛkṣa*– which leads us from one level to another and finally to the state of *Brahmānanda*, an experience that takes place only in *Samādhi*, which is indescribable, untranslatable, and non-transmutable. In this sense, Yoga is a great art, an integral art.

Man has gained political independence, material progress and all splendours of life. We have plans, schemes, hopes and visions. We are continuously striving. We are making sacrifices and marching forward, yet, strangely enough, or paradoxically, we are not progressing in real sense. Amidst plenty of material progress, we are despondent, desperate, selfish, and vanity stricken. We are continuously caught up in turmoil, violence and insecurity. The real threat to man comes from man himself, and not from any animal or alien force. That threat is the threat to his very existence. The challenges are many. The crisis that man is facing is the crisis of values.

The question is how to establish social justice, equality and brotherhood? Yoga provides answers to these questions and a way out of turmoil. It says man himself is the root cause of all evils and ills in the society. It is the mind, the inner in sanitary state, when expressed affects our social life, it helps breed the unhealthy conditions of violence and sorrow all around in our national life. Yoga purifies this inner in sanitary state. It teaches how to rediscover the greater personality in him. This art of self-discovery is the quintessence of Yoga. So, in every sense, Yoga promotes individual happiness, which in turn affects peace and happiness in social life. Yoga thus is a greater art of social reconstruction.

Chapter XI

The differences cited in the preceding pages are marginal and technical but not deep and profound. The doctrinal differences are on the surface but not too deep to drive a wedge between the two systems. After all the two systems had their origin in India – the land of spirituality. The Yoga system has remained in India but the Zen had taken its shape and form from the Mahāyāna sect of Buddhism which had been forced to trek its path in the mountain regions of Tibet, China, Korea and the far east, thus becoming the adopted son of these lands. Whatever, the historical reasons might be the two systems have immensely contributed to the peace and happiness of humanity in the world, making their presence more explicitly with redoubled vigour and will in the modern world than have ever been in the past. The systems have become more relevant than they were in the past. The one Yoga has remained firmly rooted in the native soil much against the vagaries of hostile historical weather for centuries, taking the upper hand over all other Vedāntic systems by sheer virtue of its scientific character more than its being traditional. It is a matter of pride for India that it is now penetrating into the Western hemisphere as much as Buddhism centuries ago in the far east in the form of Zen, regardless of its purity being maintained. Like Zen, Yoga is taking its multiple simplified shapes in the West to suit the fast changing life styles of man. Both systems however have become more viable, dynamic, adaptable, resilient, creative but powerful and humble.

REFERENCES

1. P.V. Bapat, *2500 Years of Buddhism*, p. 215.
2. D.T. Suziki. *Essays in Zen Buddhism*, Part I, pp. 189-190.
3. C. Alexander Simpkins. *Simple Zen*, p. 13.
4. *Ibid.*
5. Seung Sahn. *Only Don't Know* (Cumberland, R.I: Primary Points Press, 1987), p. 99.
6. Huko Yokoi. *Zen Master Dogen*, (New York: 1990), p. 84.
7. K. Mahadevan et.al. *The Glory of Indian Heritage* (New Delhi : B.R. Publishing Corporation, 1998), p. 231.
8. Shunryu Suzuki. *Zen Mind, Beginner's Mind*, (New York, Weather hill, 1971,) pp. 32-33.
9. D.T. Suzuki. *The Training of the Zen Buddhist Monk*. (Boston: Charles E. Juttle Co. Inc., 1994), p. 58.
10. *The Middle Way* (London: May 1991), p. 17.
11. Chang Chen Chi. *The Practice of Zen* (New York : Harper Brothers, 1959), pp. 28-29.
12. C. Alexander Simpkins, *Simple Zen* (Dublin: New Leaf), p. 56.

13. *Simple Zen*, p. 57.
14. D.T. Suzuki. *The Zen Koan as a Means of Attaining Enlightenment* (Boston: Charles E. Tuttle Co. Inc.,) p. 81.
15. R.F. Sasaki. *The Zen Koan* (Sau Diego : Harcourt Brace Jovanovich Publishers), p. XI.
16. Burton Watson. *The Zen Teachings of Master Lin-Chi* (Boston : Shambala), p. 99.
17. R. Pine. *The Zen Teaching of Bodidharma* (San Franḍois: North Point Press, 1989), p. 49.
18. Saraki, R.F., *The Recorded Sayings of Chian Master Lin-chi Hui-Chao of Chen Prefecture,* (Kyoto, Japan: The Institute of Zen Studies, 1975), p. 25.
19. Herregel, G. *Zen in the Art of Flower Arrangement* (London: Arkana, 1958), p. xiii.

Bibliography

Abe, M.ed. *A Zen Life : D.T. Suzuki, Remembered*. New York: Weather Hill, 1986.

Conze, E., I. Horner, D. Snellgrove and A. Waley, eds. *Buddhist Texts Through the Age*, Oxford, Engl.: One World Publications, 1995.

Das Gupta, S., *Yoga as Philosophy and Religion*, Kolkata, 1973.

Das Gupta, S., *A Study of Patañjali*, Kolkata, 1920.

Digambarji, Swami and M.L. Gharote, *Gheraṇḍa Saṁhitā*, Lonavala: Kaivalyadhama S.M. Y.M., Samiti, 1978.

Dumoulin, H. *Zen Buddhism: A History*, Vol. 1, New York, Macmillan Publishing Co., 1988.

Dumoulin, H., *Zen Buddhism: A History*, Vol. 2, New York: Macmillan Publishing Co., 1990.

Dvivedi, M.N., *The Yoga Sūtras of Patañjali*, Adyar, Chennai, 1934.

Eliade, M., *Yoga: Immortality and Freedom*, Princeton, 1973.

Feverstein, G., *The Essence of Yoga*, London, 1924.

Flagg, W.J., *Yoga or Transformation*, New York and London, 1998.

Greham, A., *Conversations: Christian and Buddhist Encounters in Japan*, New York : Harcourt Brace World. Inc.

Hall, E. *The Dance of Life*, New York : Anchor Press, Doubleday, 1983.

Hemigel, E., *The Method of Zen*, New York: Vintage Books, 1971.

Hirai, T., *Psychophysiology of Zen*. Tokyo: Igakushoin, 1974.

Jha, G. *The Yoga-Darśana*, Bombay, 1907.

Parulski, G., *A Path to Oriental Wisdom*, Burbank, Calif: Ohara Publications, Co., Inc., 1976.

Pine, R., *The Zen Teaching of Bodhidharma*. Sanfransico: North Point Press, 1989.

Prabhavananda, Swami, *Patañjali Yoga Sūtras*, Chennai: Ramakrishna Math, 2002.

Prabhavananda, Yogi, *Pure Yoga*. New Delhi: Motilal Banarasidas Publishers Pvt., Ltd., 1992.

Price, A.F. and W. Mov-lan., *The Diamond Sūtra and the Sūtra of Hui-Neng*. Boston: Shambala, 1990.

Pross,, N.W., *The World of Zen*, New York Vintage, 1960.

Saraki, R.F., *The Zen Koan*, San Diego: Harcourt Brace Jovanovich Publishers, 1965.

Shree Purohit Jawami, *Aphorisms of Yoga*, London, 1938.

Simpkins, C.A and A.M. Simpkins, *Principles of Meditation: Eastern Wisdom for the Western Mind*, Boston:Charles E. Tuttle Co. Inc., 1996.

Simpkins, C.A *Living Meditation: From Principle to Practice*, Boston, Charles E. Tuttle Co. Inc., 1997.

Simpkins, C.A., *Zen Around the World: A 2500 Year Journey from the Buddha to You*, Boston: Charles E. Tuttle Co. Inc., 1997.

Singh, L.A. *Yoga Psychology: Methods and Approaches*, Varanasi, 1940.

Suzuki, D.T. *Studies in Zen*, New York : Philosophical Library, 1955.

Suzuki, D.T., *The Zen Koan as a Means of Attaining Enlightenment*, Boston: Charles E. Tuttle Co. Inc., 1994.

Suzuki, D.T., *Zen and Japanese Culture*, Princeton, N.J.: Princeton University, 1973.

Suzuki, D.T., *The Zen Doctrine of No-Mind*, York Beach : Samet Weiser, Inc., 1972.

Suzuki, S., *Zen Mind, Beginners Mind*, New York: Wealther Hill, 1979.

Taimni, I.K., *Glimpses into the Psychology of Yoga*. Chennai: The Theosophical Publishing House, 1973.

Taimni, I.K., *The Science of Yoga*, Chennai: the Theosophical Publishing House, 1961.

Watson, Burton, *The Zen Teachings of Master Lin-Chi*, Boston: Shambala, 1993.

Yokoi, Huko, *Zen Master Dogen*, New York, Weather Hill, 1990.

Index